To Be or Not

I want to be a writer, I think but I can't tell
The life is full of dos and don'ts shall I what the hell
From manuscript to publishing, it can take many years
Now I know why writers are skint and near to tears
They work by day; they work by night, work when words do flow
People say its easy, "come on then have a go"
I did discover writing, did it discover me?
My aim in life if I'm quick, a best seller before my tea

The christening

I'm being christened a real big day
All the family gathers round oh so proud they say
All dressed up in lovely clothes then there's not a sound
I don't think its funny why am I being drowned?

All at sea

We're on the top or under the surface
Sometimes we think does life have a purpose
But it's our job and is plain to see
We're all a part of, the Navy

People think that it's a big lark
Our job is one big stroll in the park
You wouldn't think that if you were on deck
With a force ten gale blowing round your neck

A floating country and first on scene
If there's a conflict to intervene
The very first stop in the line of supply
Some keep the aircraft up in the sky

Not on our own, close to the sea bed
Our faithful submariners keep watch over head
At times near the surface in hostile warfare
An exorcet missile they put in the air

Merchant vessels keep up supply
Food and some drink, then get some shut eye
When duty is over its all steam ahead
To our wives and our family, a good night in bed

Seventies Stag do

The night before the wedding, what a good do
Out with the lads a skin full or two
A few games of pool down at the pub
Gather together then off to a club

I'm not getting legless, just have a few
If I'm rough tomorrow, what a t'do
Although in good hands, says my best man
Look out for myself, I think the best plan

It started off easy the beer it did flow
From the pub to the club then a curry you know
The party's got smaller a few lads have trapped
Those days are now over my knuckles well rapped

I'm up in the morning, I missed the bad head
Unlike my best man, he's looking half dead
A good hearty breakfast sees him on his feet
He's got lots to do, friends and family to greet

3

My Big Dream

My aim in life for when I retire
A place in the sun my only desire
I saved and saved through my working life
For something of comfort for me and the wife

They say it's so easy the kids are all gone
The brochures and adverts on telly are on
Tell you it's simple and we help all we can
Take a trip over and look at the plan

Off to the site construction is rife
Faze one two and three, are lived in and nice
Look at the pool, gym, golf course are there
Apartments or houses we don't really care

My wife sees a house that suits her to bits
A four bedroom plot sea views like the Ritz
She talks of the family when they come to stay
All her friends will never be away

We jump on the bus to look at plot four
The salesman is good "This would be the front door"
Round to the back "The pool would be there
Picture yourselves with a drink in a chair"

4

"Sign on the line and pay a deposit"
"The property's yours if you really want it"
A few little questions I hastened to ask
"Has the planning gone through and everything passed?"

"No worries on that" the agent did say
"Save small little details for some other day
Just pay the price, and secure up the plot
Solicitors fees, they won't cost a lot"

Back to the hotel to speak to the wife
She thought it lovely and I thought it nice
But being belts and braces my thinking head on
No planning permission, was this the one?

So back to England a near miss I fear
Foreign home problems on the news we do hear
Rain on the window sat in my chair
We'll just have a holiday a few times a year

The Brass Band

I'm going to a concert to see a Brass Band
There's twenty eight players they don't half sound grand
Bass and Euphonium, baritone trombone
The meat of the band a deep soul full tone
Horns and the flugal, cornets and sop
I meant the soprano they're always on top
Let's not forget percussion the bands engine room
All steered by the conductor in a sweet sounding tune
Allsorts of pieces songs from the shows
Marches and operas the odd overtures
Then there's the test piece to drive the band nuts
Rehearse for the contest and play with some guts
It all seems so stressful but anyone can tell
A shield or a trophy the bands done so well

Fighter plane

We flew the planes of battle the enemy from the sun
Dive and turn over the loop and then you hit the gun
Once in battle, it happened so fast, there's no time to look
A volley of fire dive right down and enemy plane I took

Back to base on the ground relax and take it steady
The plane is always hanger bound the ground crew make it ready
Debriefing time the notes all made to verify a kill
No time to waste the group phone rings you always feel a chill

We've been stood down no urgent threat a break in their retreat
To the billet have a wash, drink, and grab some sleep
The shout goes out "squadron ready" kit up, and by the phone
The wait seems long, but here we go the ringing piercing tone

On the run, aircraft ready airborne one by one
In formation gain some height attacking from the sun
The dog fight starts, watch your back, leader wing man break
Planes of battle returning home killing in their wake

Be Green

Use public transport, the watch word for years
Those who say, should try it, they'd soon be near to tears
Go, by the underground, train or a bus
At rush hour time, folk about, it's always a push

Underground,......Train, rush hour on your feet
I wouldn't really mind, but I paid for a seat
Stop at a station, more getting on
Push and shove your way off, or your station gone

Onto the bus, not much change there
Now you've paid, the driver won't care
Off like a rocket brake the next stop
Bum's off the seats, back down they flop

Swings round the corner throw us about
The station is there shell shocked and we're out
Use public transport say those at the top
I'm back in the car the nightmare will stop

Lady killers

Shopping the one thing, you know we're the best
We sniff out the bargains and barge out the rest
If we spot something, on that big rail
Keep out of the way if it's in the sale

Sometimes we're cunning and grab up the lot
Then sort out the good stuff, away from the grot
But there's an odd time when the garment has gone
We hope it's too tight and it's back when tried on

You turn out a stalker when pushed, if you fail
If you lose that item you spot on the rail
A doubt on that face, it's time to move in
It could mean the item is prey once again

The garment is moving, back into stock
Weigh up the comp like a kestrel you clock
Just an inch more, and back on the rail
Grab it up quick, this time you don't fail

Off to the till to tot it all up
Bruised and all battered by the risks that you took
"Hanger' and rage all soon fade away
"Look at the money I've saved here today!"

9

Why do nothing

We talk of the planet and things out in space
Look we're creating a climate disgrace
The ozone depleted from the suns blazing rays
Life of the planet decreasing by days

Sea level's rising eating up ground
Ice caps are melting what we have found
The carbon emissions, power stations and cars
Add to the problem we know that is ours

Solar and wind, hydro power too
Planet protectors that's what we should do
Try to cut down on the old fossil fuel
It needs to be done or we'll be the fool

Let's try to slow down before it's too late
Look to the future past problems can wait
Pool altogether the knowledge we've got
Governments together help stop the rot

Stop all the testing below the sea bed
We've started in space more problems I dread
So let's make the effort and sort this mess out
We'll be the loser in that there's no doubt

Take Care for Christmas

Merry Christmas to you all
Drink and eat, have a ball
You've ate to much, and can't go
Monastery herbs will help you know
You had to push down one more sprout
To try to help the problem out
But in the end a Senerkot
Will surely blow away the lot
So happy new year, when it comes be merry
You don't want a bum like a Christmas cherry

I've done that (just sixty)

A bloke I once knew, he was a one
Said he fought in world war two, at the Soome
It couldn't be him, he would have been three
When world war two ended, he'd be on his mum's knee

Ran with the hard men but never got caught
Done national service in Suez he fought
Professional football, Cricket and swim
Boxed at all weights, well known down the gym

Plumber, Pub Landlord, Bricky and Chef
Train and Bus driver Plane captain a Ref
Stood in on a lifeboat, crew short on a shout
In rough seas and gales pulled twenty two out

Paint like Picasso, a Waterhouse glade
Pencil and water in oil, sculpture made
Garden designer, house, --- built a few
Doctor and Dentist, an Explorer too

There's no quiet moment when he's in full flow
Talking of life and his tales long ago
Have you in laughter and some time in tears
A real entertainer can roll back the years

We've lost the use of common sense

In days gone by when things cropped up
We did not panic and dive for a book
The computers tell if things are there
But if they're not were in despair
We find it hard to comprehend
We're told one way and can't bend

Keep death off the road

Walking the pavements like walking the plank
A dangerous occupation if I'm really frank
Bike's flying by, like a menace appear
Loud personal hifi as it whizzed by my ear
If a cars turning right and a junction is blocked
You have to look out on the pavement I clocked
The lights of a car with no time to wait
Pavements a jungle with people as bait

Make a Family

Go back forty years or more
We stuck together, be rich or poor
Divorce was frowned at, if it didn't last
Nods and whispers when people passed

But now it's nothing in life today
Single parents make their way
If things get tough, we just split
Social services cover it

A quick way round to get a flat
Teenagers pregnant, easy as that
Boy friends not there all of the week
It makes for rent free-- now that's a cheek

All too young the kids today
Live life too fast and throw it away
Their early years have just begun
They should be out and having fun

The years fly by as you get old
Responsibility grows, --- be told
So take things slow in your early life
It's a serious thing being Man and Wife

Volunteer, we'll make things better

Canals and towpaths, have been run down
Industrial heritage from town to town
Years ago they became a tip
Till volunteers put a stop to it

Teams started off to make things good
Then the government thought, it's time they should
Regenerate, our industrial age
Make houses, apartments that's all the rage

Big business jumped, on the gravy train
In towns and cities, old industrial drain
Buy up a mill, in some derelict place
Old docks and canals, make money at pace

Water board replace, tunnel, lock and bridge
Build up the bank, dredge out the odd fridge
Make waterways free, for the holiday trade
Town's new marina, the council has paid

Hold up now what's that in my ear
The governments cutting the grants we fear
Don't tell us that now, after all the works done
With the cuts that are due we'll be back to square one

You can't pick your neighbours

We've lived in this street for twenty odd years
A new home to live in, excited no fears
Neighbours let on, the odd cup of tea
Chat in the garden, plod on merrily
A new fence erected the old one well done
Consult with the neighbours about the new one
Put in the new panels paint them to suit
Every one happy, to go down that route

On completing the fence, a problem I fear
One side complain of the height we do hear
"We don't mind the first two, panels that high
We're out of the picture and wondering why"
"If height of the fence is a problem for you
It's because of the slope of the land that is true
The main road and traffic the problem you see
Now in the summer we're private for tea"

Then it all started the odd thing at first
We found a few tacks, a car tyre it did burst
Then chips , and scratches on the side of the car
Door mirror bent, it is getting bizarre
Branches cut off, and over the fence
Hose pipe and stones, he's lost common sense
Gutter and flashing the conservatory top
CCTV, this just has to stop

At first with no proof, and a shadow of doubt
Caught on TV "Got him" I shout
The answer was there straight in our face
Neighbour from hell what a disgrace
Evidence gathered, write out a log
CCTV, this was a long slog
Near two years pass by, of bricks and abuse
The police are called in, a warning cut loose

All the way through, my wife oh so strong
She's been the main aim of attack all too long
Let's hope it's the end of those menacing days
'Is the neighbour from hell? ', mending his ways
We won't hold our breath, too fast this year
It needs two or three to be well in the clear
His long reign of terror we hope now will end
Don't make a neighbour a mate or a friend

I only want a bit

My thingies broke; I need a part it won't be hard to fit
I'll save my cash, and DIY, it only needs a bit
The old parts here, a rubber washer to keep the water in
I'll take it with me, being smart, won't throw it in the bin

A quick phone call to check for stock, "come down we'll have one here"
Jump in the car, nip into town, inside a little cheer
Join the queue, won't be long, the staff they know their stuff
I'm at the front, and in my bag, the part I know is duff

"Ok pal lets have a look and see what can be done"
Part book out, computer on, the look, you know the one
"You'll have to buy all this for it" "I only want that bit"
"The parts don't come in ones no more you have to buy a kit"

So off back home big bag in hand inside there's parts galore
Pulled all out, take to bits, all on the kitchen floor
There it is, the washer, that cost me thirty quid
Now I have a bag of parts, I'll keep and won't get rid

But knowing my luck they'll never be used, just left there in the bag
The part I need not worth 10p these shops know how to blag
No labour charge no call out fee for some one to fix it
Really,--- it costs you just as much, when you only what a bit

18

Credit card cappers

Long time ago, when I first came out I was thorough of something
  special
In my place, in the wallet I sit, at the front of the notes worth mi metal
But now I'm afraid, a piece of plastic thrown in with six or seven
  brothers
With no special place in the spending race, used and abused like the
others

I can go weeks, when my credit rate peaks just sat in the dark there's
  no doubt
But like all the rest, I feel I'm the best ,when I'm called for and have to
  get out
Wiz through a machine or stuffed up an hole, my pin number punched
  in above
Now I'm number one, for the next few days the card they're beginning
  to love

All of a sudden no movement for days, this time we hate in the year
The credit card statement has flopped on the mat, on the table lined
shaking with fear
Over spent, no room to manoeuvre, all limits are reached everyone
Consolidate debt, they say they regret, chop down to two, or just one
On the table in bits, the cold steel rips, through the hart of a few
  of the cards
Alive in the dark, I'm saved what a lark--- in credit,---- still worth mi
metal

The recipe for a big bang

We've been raped and pillaged for many a year
Our country in turmoil does the government care
Social services bleeding to death
Hospitals are poorly, and near their last breath
The thin blue line is all but gone
No law in the classroom generation time bomb
Out on the streets people in fear
Stay in their homes dark days of the year
Transport depleted no reasonable care
Unscrupulous companies buyers beware
Home life ruined, family apart
Bosses squeeze money from the workforce at heart
Taxed to the hilt funds leaking so fast
A time bomb created, how long before the blast?

The Stage

Live entertainment is dieing fast
The concert halls were built to last
But sadly we find they're in decay
Audiences seem to stay away

It's only September

Well all the moaners, I have to agree
Things come too early, for you, and for me
While out on a walk at weekend I spot
January sales start at this here car lot

I called in the shops, and to my despair
Christmas in lights, with cards, wrap all there
On the next isle, I'm spooked by a ghost
With Halloween pumpkins and bats as a host

A report in the paper at a house they are seen
5000 lights, make a big Christmas scene
So Happy New Year, get your Valentine teddy
Don't be too late get your Easter egg ready

Say the word, Its Cancer

This thing has come inside me, no one really knows
Where it exactly comes from, or where it really goes
It's really got a grip of me I'm feeling awful rough
The doc he said "that's nothing" the 'medson mighty tough

The fight is on let's go for it and give it all we've got
Some days with all the side effects I feel as I've been shot
There's times when we are lucky, caught in an early stage
With surgery and medicine, we can hold back the rage

We strive to find a cure for this, research work in the lab
Days we feel we're lucky, and others drive us mad
Genes and body chemistry things that make us tick
As if we press a self destruct our body plays a trick

Sometimes the primary's never found this knocks us to the floor
Its only at this moment, we look at heavens door
We're thankful for the hospitals and secondary support
Time to leave our family, in this life we abort

We all know, the fight goes on, and it will never drop
But until then we carry on a cure we hope we'll stop
This thing inside that cuts us down and no respect for age
Fight it through, be the boss, decide your own last page

Bonfire Night

We've done all the logging the bunties built up
We've got a spare pile in case some of it's took
You have to be careful at this time of year
Some of your wood can soon disappear

The guy is all ready to sit on the top
All fireworks in tins we bought from the shop
As it goes dark we light up the fire
The night has begun the flames getting higher

A sparkler is lit to draw in the dark
Light someone else's from the last dying spark
One of the dads starts up the display
Lit one by one it takes longer this way

Parkin, treacle toffee, hot pot and hot dogs
Belly near to burst as we sit on some logs
Swilling it down with orange and pop
"Look a roman candle", fizz" that was a flop"

Nowhere to sit, the last wood thrown on
The last jacket spud in silver foil gone
Not many left to watch out the fire
A small little pile as the embers retire

Christmas past and present

Christmas time was a time of year
When the hustle and bustle would just disappear
Two days before we'd do the last shop
At four Christmas Eve things came to a stop

Shops are still open till eight Christmas Eve
Now Christmas day on the cards we believe
Why are we greedy, why can't things stop?
The true meaning of Christmas, have we forgot?

Home from work to get everything ready
Hot mince pie from the oven comes steady
Make a few extra there'll be knocks at the door
Brass bands, singers and carols galore

In from work burnt out with the pace
Quick tidy round in life's hectic race
Presents all packed thrown under the tree
Beer wine and spirits for missus and me

Kids all soon ready, up off to bed
Dreaming of Santa's sleigh in their head
Stockings all packed and put by the fire
A beer and a sherry then up to retire

"Its gone half passed one, you should be in bed
Open your presents in the morning I said"
Its soon ten o clock in the morning I fear
I'm working the Boxing Day sales this year

At six in the morning we hear the first stir
Then "Has he been?" and a noise on the stair
Got to get up the excitement and fun
Yes Christmas day, finally has come

The latest technology covers the floor
Up to the bedroom to pack in some more
One hundred pound trainers, come down the stairs
"My mates on the mobile I'm off round to theirs"

Open the door to the house and we see
Stocking by the fire and a dressed well lit tree
Presents of clothes, slippers and choc's
Rag doll and a flashlight in its own separate box

The table is set its gone half past three
Hundred plus stations on this plasma TV
We're all round the table a first for the year
Meals on a rota is normal round here

While the children all play with the toys by the tree
The table is set for the whole family
Dinner at one, wash up, Queen on at three
Pick the big film ITV, BBC

Christmas day over but more still to come
A time for the family relaxing and fun
Work in the morning sales start at ten
Christmas is over on the tread mill again

The Heron

I'll stand here so still so I won't be seen
At the edge of this pond the sun warm in its beam
The fish all glide by I won't even budge
I'll wait for a big one before the water I nudge

My beak fully open as quick as a flash
The fish nearly see me, and put on a dash
Crash in the water a large shoal so near
One fish for my breakfast, as I pull my beak clear

My snack had, and over, I'll leave the pond now
Making my way, follow, river or canal
As I fly over houses the odd garden pond
I pinch a few fish if the net's not so strong

The canal, on the towpath I ponder and sit
A fish up for air, quickly, grab it
I'd sit here all day but for people about
Keep on the move when the camera comes out

My life as a heron, not much to shout
I do like it best when no ones about
I don't cause much trouble and not often seen
But where there's a fish, in my eye there's a gleam

How old is that

When we woke this morning we where feeling really grand
Knew that it would not be long to hold your little hand
Although a thirty something, young and very bold
But now, a **granddad and grandma,** another generation old

Coming of age

Twenty one years the key to the door
I had one at six don't mean much no more
We grow up so fast childhood has gone
The most I can say is, I'm twenty one

Small crumbs

The world is a stage a massive big play
With leaders and governments with plenty to say
It's not a rehearsal life can be tough
We just have to take the smooth with the rough